A
BLANKET
OF
RAVEN FEATHERS

A
BLANKET
OF
RAVEN FEATHERS

POEMS

By
Larry Schug

NORTH STAR PRESS OF ST. CLOUD, INC.
St. Cloud, Minnesota

ISBN: 978-1-68201-071-6

First edition: May 2017

Printed in the United States of America.
This book is printed on 100% post-consumer recycled content.

Published by
North Star Press
19485 Estes Road
Clearwater, MN 55320
www.northstarpress.com

Acknowledgements

The following poems have been originally published in these print and online literary journals.

"Another Place Called Heaven" and "While Reading Ferlinghetti" in *Diverse Voices*.

"Approaching Sharon Springs" and "Change" in *The Talking Stick*.

"Doll" in *Cats With Thumbs*.

"Another Starry Night," "Between La Jara and Romeo," and "The God of Dumb Luck" in *Hobo Camp Review*.

"Small" and "At Recovery Plus" in *A Little Poetry*.

"A Toothache During the Bombing of Baghdad" and "Diamonds" in *Social Justice Poetry*.

"Bait and Switch" and "Peaches" in *Your Daily Poem*.

"Encounter with a Collared Lizard," "Worm," "Someone Who Carries the Sun," and "Noon" in *Shot Glass Journal*.

"What Would She Think of Poetry" and "Womb" in *Phree Write Magazine*.

"As If We Were Not Brothers" in *Deep Waters Journal*.

"Good-Bye, Mojo," "This is the day the apple tree lost its blossoms," and "Rendezvous at the Apple Dumpling Stand" in *Poetry Quarterly*.

"Memorials of Plastic Flowers," "Irregular," My Buddy's Girlfriend," and "Bluebird on the Roof" in *Eye on Life Magazine*.

"Advice for a Road Trip" in *The Poet Community*.

"Eve," "Mother Milkweed," "One Evening in Santa Fe," and "Two Ravens" in *Studio 1*.

"Feeding the Birds in a Blizzard" in *Poeming Pigeons Anthology* (2014).

"El Rio del Oso" in *The Café Review*.

"Clean Fill," "The Other Side of the Night," "Shell," "I Imagine Rabbits," "A Cacophony of Crows," "Three Sandhill Cranes," "Migration Variations," "Minnesota's No Different," "Clay," "If We Make it to Willmar," "Connection," "Raffle," "My Old Friend Jack," "Antiques," and "Air Raid Drill" in *Obsessed With Mud* (Poetry Harbor, 1997).

"Vultures" in *Artword Quarterly*.

"When a Jenny Wren," "Cosmic Bread Recipe," and "Calvary Cemetery, 1962" in *An Amazing Eclectic Anthology* (2016).

Dedication

Finding Jacob, Finding Alayna, Losing Everything

Life itself seems ludicrous,
the sun shining on the forest floor,
light filtered by shimmering aspen leaves
on grass seemingly dancing in the wind,
so achingly lovely
at a time broken hearts must bear up the sky,
a time when light fails to illuminate
the darkness that seeps into the soul,
and even love, the greatest of all gifts,
like sunlight given way to night,
brings blindness to eyes
searching for some kind of reason
in a world that makes no sense.
And yet, love and light are all we have.

Table of Contents

I

II

III

IV

V

VI

I

a day as three paintings

robin's breast of dawn
lights the pink-stained glass
of a rabbit's ears

sun a honeybee
sky a blue dragonfly
hover above a meadow
of black-eyed susans

night's caress
a blanket
of raven feathers

Be Mindful of the Honeybee

As you eat your homemade apple pie,
while sipping tea with honey sweetened,
be mindful of the apples,
the leaves that made your tea.
Be mindful of the honeybee
that pollinated your apple tree last spring,
buzzing apple blossoms
that delight your every sense,
turning them into round red globes,
the apples of your eye,
as well as your teeth and tongue
and tummy, especially as pie.
And that's not the end of it, my friend.
The apple tree's miracle
is making oxygen for you to breathe
and in which the honeybee swims.
Good ol' O_2,
you need it,
you want it,
you got to have it.
It gives you a buzz
like a honeybee's hum,
though you might hear it as a hymn,
a song of thanks,
with which you can hum along
and make into your own sweet song.

Another Place Called Heaven

I'm sitting on the front porch steps,
barefoot on a late summer afternoon,
dog lying beside me,
his golden fur luxurious in my hands.
The lawn, freshly mown,
fills my nose with a sweet smell
and I can't hear an engine anywhere,
only the sound of you in the kitchen
chopping green garden peppers for supper.
A cool breeze from the north
keeps the mosquitoes away
and a hundred helicopter dragonflies,
indigo blue and fire engine red,
maneuver through the air in impossible patterns.
Bumblebees and migrating monarchs
flit between marigolds and black-eyed susans.
The birches and maples show the first hint
of impending autumn glory.
A cardinal, three raucous blue jays
and a flock of goldfinches
finish the sunflower seeds in the feeders
as a small red squirrel with a white belly
chatters angrily down at them from a whispering aspen.
We have plans for making love tonight.
It's hard to believe in another place called heaven
that you must die to enter.

A Roof Above Your Head

A romantic realist such as Thoreau
or a magical realist such as García Márquez,
unable to fend off fate
or rain
might say to a tree
thank you for allowing me to murder you
in order to put a roof over my mortal head.
To which a cynical but congenial tree,
as valuable as a metaphor
as it is as a roof beam, might reply
that, though I, with my brothers and sisters,
gave you every breath you've ever breathed
you murdered me for momentary expediency
and possess the audacity
to write your poems on my dead skin.
Well, breathe as long as you can,
you romantic pissant fool.
I'll be a roof beam a hundred more years.
You'll be nothing more than evaporated tears.

Your Mother

If you saw her on some dirty sidewalk,
her shopping cart overflowing
with feathers and roots,
shiny stones and snowflakes,
a bag of oxygen, water, and soil,
drops of dew reflecting the universe,
you might think her a crazy woman
with nowhere to go.
If you look at her closely, though,
you would see the smile she hides
on a face both youthful and ancient,
a blessed serenity behind wrinkled eyelids.
If you stopped to admire her treasures,
she would offer them all to you,
a cure for the sickness and mean-spiritedness
you carry on your back.
If you accept her gifts with good grace,
she'll invite you to a dance danced in moonlight,
the music of the spheres moving you in ways
you've never been moved before.
You might treat her as if she's your mother.
She is.

Mother Milkweed

Whispy white hair blowing wild
as milkweed silk,
more beautiful than she's ever been,
she thinks back to the May of her life
among black-eyed susans, blue-eyed grass,
chamomile and clover,
how she held a chrysalis then,
as only one who's been chosen
by a fluttering, floating life
can hold a fluttering, floating life.

The Monarch Deposed

All it takes for anarchy to reign
is clear-cutting forests of oyamel fir
in Mexico's Sierra Nevada,
scything down, poisoning,
plowing under the humble milkweeds
of America's farm lands.
Add a change in climate
and the butterflies are gone forever,
vanishing like fallen maple leaves,
absorbed by the soil that claims all life.
Unlike the fall of human kings,
there is no joy
when this benevolent monarch is deposed,
not replaced by democracy, but one-party rule,
a dictatorship of man
on naked mountains,
endless fields of hybrid corn.

Palos Verdes Blue

Whether you're caged in a cubicle,
alone in a dark house, curtains drawn,
strapped in a wheelchair,
sheltered at night beneath a bridge
or a poet unread,
you might think you'd like to be
a being with wings,
perhaps a Palos Verdes Blue butterfly,
floating above grassy dunes beside the sea,
by a miracle, no longer endangered,
treasured by eyes, wide with wonder
at the you that is you.

Before the Prairie Disappears

Mourning cloaks and swallowtails
roost in the heart of the world.
In the cool of evening, wings flutter,
silently fold into stillness
like hands fold into prayer.
Black-eyed susans and blue-eyed grass
bow their heads in the purple gloaming
like the cloistered Sisters of Poor Clare
whispering vespers.

Clean Fill

Like endless, mindless tv shows
clot the terrain of thoughtful thinking,
another beeping dump truck backs up
to another chirping wetland,
silences singing insects and frogs,
breaks buried turtle eggs
and flattens a bed of fluffy cattails.
The truck lets loose a landslide
of Pleistocene landscape,
laced with leaked oil and construction debris,
the amputated roots of maples and elms,
fallen bird nests and broken butterfly wings—
all classified as "clean fill,"
filling another little swamp clean full.

A Better Place to Die

Another dead raccoon,
a pool of blood dripped from its mouth,
not an unusual sight on a country road,
though when I encounter these carcasses
I stop and place the bodies in the ditch
among wild violets and bloodroot
to honor their existence in this world,
knowing they once breathed the same air I breathe.

After dragging this particular corpse to the roadside,
I tell it I am sorry about people and cars,
all the havoc humans create in this world;
in my way, trying to bless its life
with a better place to die,
when I notice its silky fur moving,
its belly shallowly rising and falling,
its eyes opening with a mere squint.

I can't breathe. I'm trembling.
I don't know what to do.
With no way to end its suffering,
other than running it over or bashing it's head with a rock,
I leave the raccoon in the ditch, its fate in the unseen hands
of whatever god, if any, that decides about life and death
in the world of raccoons, skunks, and squirrels,
hoping it might survive, somehow resurrect
to once again roam farm fields and woodlots,
soft fur glistening with morning's dew.
A doubtful scenario,
it being likely that when I return to this place

the body will be already reincarnated, transformed
from a rotting pile of fur and guts and gnawed bones,
into a new life as a mouse or cawing crow,
but thinking that if I had a choice,
I would willingly surrender my body
to crows and coyotes and field mice,
to insects cleaning my bones so they shine in moonlight,
though, most likely, I'll have to be satisfied
that my cremated remains might provide nourishment
to a single blood-red wild rose,
so full of its little life, it glows.

The Other Side of the Night

The road is an obituary page I read on the way to work,
listing the names of skunks and raccoons and squirrels
who failed to reach the other side of the night,
green eyes blinded by the beams of passing headlights.
Crows pick through the crumpled clothes of the dead
like raucous shoppers finding good deals
among the garments of the deceased at the Goodwill store.
Rush-hour traffic dims its lights as the sun rises
and fog dissipates like departing souls;
drivers like myself swerve around the carcasses
as if death can be avoided.

Shell

I paddle up close to the corpse,
half-fascinated, half-afraid;
a dead body is a dead body, after all,
whether it wears feathers or skin.
This dead body wears a shell
big around as a trash can lid,
crusty with black algae
peeling like a birch tree's hide.

The snapper's head hangs limp
at the end of its outstretched neck,
mouth open, steel-trap jaws slack
beneath murky water,
claws large as a wolf's,
reaching for either life or death
as if it makes no difference;
both appealing as a log floating
on sun-shimmering water.

I paddle back to shore,
wondering how I will protect my life spark
without a hard shell, long claws,
no way to clamp down on anything for long.

I Imagine Rabbits

Nuthatches cling upside down
to a slippery aspen in my daydream;
chickadees fly into my head,
grab a seed, fly away again.
The blue jay boys raise a ruckus,
but even they quiet
when the hawk's shadow
glides over the snow.
Sparrows freeze,
make themselves small;
no way to tell
who redtail will choose today.
I tuck my head under my wing,
pretend I am invisible.

At night in bed
I lie on my back, imagine rabbits
nibbling contemplatively in moonlight,
rejoice awhile,
that the hawk did not choose me.
But then an owl calls,
the night hunter is about.
I know the rabbits have scattered,
but I lie awake;
many mornings I have found
a spot of blood, a tuft of fur,
imprint of wing in snow.

I Prepare to Live

I burn the dregs
of last year's woodpile,
pine chips and box elder splinters,
good enough to break the chill
of April's last morning.
I don't need to burn any oak today,
I repile it, save it for next winter.

I plant potatoes for the same reason,
I assume I'll still be here at harvest.
Call it presumption, an act of faith,
in my case, maybe just stubbornness.
I know people die with the woodshed full,
leave behind uneaten potatoes in the cellar,
sprouts crawling from closed eyes.

El Rio del Oso

What is the name of rain
when it fails to fall from a cloud

What do you call a river
no water flowing within its banks

having returned to the sky
or been swallowed by the earth

Name it a braided channel of sand
evidence of singing water
promise of another song

What do you call a tear
before it has been cried

leaving the lake of your eye
flowing down the land of your face

absorbed by your shirt sleeve
your finger dabbing it dry

Call it testimony of the heart
proof of a singing soul
covenant with life lived

Mississippi River Blues

You have to travel to Itasca to hear this river sing,
a child's song, burbling over stones.
Downriver in St. Cloud, behind the dam
the water whispers, barely audible,
riffling the branches of a fallen tree,
though it screams angry words when released
into a polluted pool of chemical run-off,
a swirling rainbow slick of wasted oil,
below a concrete spillway in the name of electricity.
From a satellite, the river's image
may seem a string of pearls if captured light is right,
but it's a necklace of stagnant puddles
imprisoned by locks and dams,
a slave to human industry.
Oh, Father of Waters, mistreated Mother of Life,
how could it be otherwise that the blues of Memphis,
the blues of Natchez and New Orleans,
were birthed in the fields along your shackled banks.

Dragonfly

While reading in the shade of a sugar maple,
a black-and-white dragonfly
lands on the book's black-and-white page,
lingers only a few seconds,
a speed reader, I guess,
or perhaps it finds words less important
than hunting mosquitoes on the breeze.
I try to read the dragonfly
but I read too slowly, it's gone
and I turn to a blank white page instead,
scribble black words,
thinking these poems
are much the same as dragonflies
just pausing to rest from the hunt.

Encounter with a Collared Lizard

A collared lizard,
a dinosaur in miniature,
crosses our path, stops to sun itself
on a limestone rock in a dry stream bed,
a meeting of species
that seems serendipitous, if not predestined,
even in the vast desert of space and time,
as if my human life is no accident,
but some sort of blessing,
not from the God who lives in churches,
demanding worship and sacrifice,
but from the goddess of small places and little lives,
the goddess who can't wipe the smile from her face.

The Third Day of Rain

The day I saw a snapping turtle
laying her eggs, miniature full moons,
in the gravel beside a country road,
was the third day of heavy rain—
three days and nights of gloom,
the woods, dark as dusk at noon,
yet seemingly, the perfect day
for a mossy-shelled snapper
to deposit eggs in rain-softened soil,
somehow knowing the sun
would soon shine,
warm her sandy incubator
after she returns to a boggy pond,
a lesson in faith and hope,
trust that life will unfold as it will.

Worms

Rain
beckons earthworms from the soil
to the paved surfaces
humans have seemingly grown to prefer
in place of living earth.
But having tiny brains,
no capacity to think ahead,
worms lie on this ungiving veneer,
become easy pickings for robins, tires, and feet.
Many simply shrivel in the sun,
a metaphorical message, perhaps
to creatures with complicated brains
who, nonetheless, place themselves in situations
they can't think of a way to wiggle out of.

Otters

The gods and goddesses
of this small place
open their hands,
present me with a gift—
four otters,
undulating water dancers,
slithering, sliding, glistening,
gliding through ripples
of their own making.
I'm sixty-nine years old.
I'd never seen an otter in the wild.
I may never see another,
but I watch for otters every day now,
eyes open for the open hands
that hold all the gifts
with which the gods tease us—
sunlight, air, earth, water,
and otters.

The West Wind in Minnesota

In Minnesota
the wind blows from the west today,
carrying the exhaled breaths
of Idaho and Montana ranchers,
their grazing cattle and horses,
the breaths of prairie dogs in the Dakotas,
of salmon breathing underwater
off the coasts of Washington and Oregon,
the slowly released sighs of Ponderosa pine
that have survived the summer's fires.
For all I know, the wind may be carrying
the exhalations of the Far East across the ocean.
I inhale these prevailing westerlies,
exhale as if my breath is a poem read aloud,
send it on to Wisconsin.

This is the day
the apple tree shed its blossoms

like a lady
leaving her pink-and-white gown
on an emerald lawn,
a beautiful woman
changing into a shimmering green dress,
beaded with ruby globes, summer bangles.
She's comfortable in her choice,
while the sky, a woman with too large a closet,
can't decide what to wear;
first trying on blue raiment,
adding a touch of white with a yellow accent,
then changing again into muted gray,
quickly shifting into a tie-dyed muumuu
of swirling colors, apricot, peach, tangerine,
before opting for a long black gown
accented with silver glitter,
perfect for a night on the town,
yet alluring, as she walks arm in arm
on a country lane with earth, her love.

Bait and Switch

March in Minnesota
is a salesman with a genuine smile,
a glad hand,
a pat on the shoulder, ol' buddy.
March promises you everything,
whispers in your ear
with a warm south breath,
tells you what you want to hear,
turns your head with sunshine,
assures you Spring will arrive any day now.
And you want Spring so badly—
red maple buds about to burst,
erect as an aroused lover's nipples,
purple and yellow violas underfoot,
that you buy what March sells,
and you're caught unprepared,
you feel like you've been suckered
by the truckload of snow
and a bill for its removal
that arrives on your doorstep
the following morning.

Kayak

My blue kayak,
is becalmed in golden fog.
I forget my own breath,
imagine I am floating
inside the egg
from which everything
is hatched.
I feel no urgency
to crack this horizon,
up and down matter not
in this place of unnamed colors.
Water and sky, sky and water.
I rejoice in floating.

Someone Who Carries the Sun

Though only a small hole
has opened in the ice,
the reflection
of sunlit birches
buried beneath snow all winter
floats again in open water
the way a person can emerge
from seasons of darkness,
return to light
with the help of someone
who carries the sun
in her hands.
She waits for you,
the light in her eyes a promise,
to help you find the light
you carry inside yourself,
perhaps dim, but not extinguished,
rekindle it like gently blowing on coals
to bring the fire back to life.

She Offers Her Hands to the Earth

She brings seeds of black-eyed susans,
offers them to the earth.
Earth brings sustenance
to the eyes of her spirit.

She brings seeds of beans,
offers them to the earth.
Earth brings sustenance
to the body her spirit wears.

She brings seeds of sage,
offers them to the earth.
Earth brings sustenance
in the sweetness of breathing.

She brings seeds of pumpkin,
offers them to the earth.
Earth brings sustenance
with the mystery of mystery.

She brings seeds of blue-eyed grass,
offers them to the earth.
Earth brings sustenance,
new life from death.

She offers her hands to the earth.

II

The Morning of April Fourth

I watch the moon's eclipse,
my dog beside me,
loyal as only a dog can be,
though he seems to be wondering
why we're standing in the old pasture
in the five a.m. darkness.

I hear a great-horned owl's cry,
in some cultures, an omen of death,
though my neighbor's rooster,
harbinger of light, crows mightily,
perhaps to halt the death of darkness
engulfing the full moon.

I find myself in the center of a metaphor;
life, death, rebirth,
a poem spoken by moon and sun and earth,
and I, feeling so cosmically small
until the dog nudges me, reminding me
that though small, I am not insignificant.

A Single Feather Floating

A small gray feather,
one of those downy underfeathers
that keep birds warm,
floats down from the sky,
gently settles on the snow.
My first thought at observing this
is to wonder if this floating feather
is one of those significant incidents,
like a butterfly flapping its wings
in the Brazilian rainforest,
sending ripples in the air
all around the world.

As far as I can tell
nothing near me but me
is affected by this feather falling,
though I have no way of knowing
if this falling feather
changed the world around you
as you walk through another day of your life.
What I do know
is in the few seconds it takes for this feather
to float by, it whispers to me,
a poem appears from the ether.
Whether or not the wind of breath expelled
when these words are spoken aloud,
will cause ripples anywhere,
I, most likely, won't know that, either,
any more than a falling feather knows its effect.
It slowly falls to earth, like all of us,
gravity, its god.

Bird Bell

Long ago in a faraway place there was a time there were no birds because the people had cut down all the trees. They said birds do not keep us warm in winter, but many kinds of birds are delicious to eat, and besides, bare mountainsides can be terraced for gardens. Is this not worth birdsong?

Not all the people felt this way. One day a bell maker, a shaper of brass, heard a lonely sparrow sing outside his window, its song a sound not heard since his youth. He shook his gray-bearded head. Has it been that long since I've heard such sweetness?

The bell maker crumbled up some crusts of bread and placed them outside his window. The sparrow found the bread, ate it and sang a song of gratitude which brought the bell maker to tears. The bell maker mixed his tears with sparrow song in a magic cauldron, cast the mixture in a mold and created a handle shaped like a sparrow for a fine brass bell. He placed the sparrow's song in the bell's clapper. The bell maker kept the bell on his window sill and rang it every day until the day he died, when the bell disappeared just as if it had flown away. Since that day the sparrows have returned, their sweet songs nesting once again in the ears of the people, who listened to them again, were grateful in their hearts and began planting trees once more.

only a poem

only a poem
owes anything

everything

to a bicycle
rusting
in the weeds
behind the pump house

a solo little sparrow
perched on handlebars

mine
the only ears
within the bell
of her song

Dance

Woodpeckers drumming a hollow elm
rap out a rhythm
that sets a hundred juncos and sparrows
to hoppin' and boppin',
each dancing their own dance,
yet dancing as one;
trippin' a free-form fandango,
that ain't no tango, bro.

A cardinal and oriole sing a duet,
mourning doves singing sweet harmony.
Warblers warble along
and when fat-boy robin chimes in
the scene gets to really rockin'
as goldfinches chip chip small talk
shuffle a little, dip into the seeds
like chaperones at a sock hop.

What can you do on a morning like this
but dance like a crazy man,
pretending there aren't too many people
on this earth mucking up everything,
that the air and water are clean,
that there no attacks on whales and wolves,
on condors or redwood trees,
that the earth is not being covered by cement
and tire tracks
that you can still hear yourself think
above the electronic cacophony
you've plugged yourself into.

Of Snowstorms, Pheasants, and Zen

I become hypnotized by falling snow,
flakes big as potato chips, wind-whipped,
filling the air like fog.
I opt to remain indoors, feed the wood stove,
sip a cup of hot Earl Grey,
read of Amado's tropical Brazil,
but I can't help but think of pheasants—
three cocks, robed in rainbow vestments,
four hens, wearing brown habits
like the simple nuns of St. Francis,
seen this morning pecking cracked corn
on the ground beneath my bird feeders;
how, in this deepening powder, they
must be hunkered in the shelter of cedar boughs
or tunneled in caves of reed canary grass in the bog,
perhaps deep inside one of the brush piles,
I stacked after cutting firewood last fall;
pheasants with no sense of time,
only darkness and light,
knowing warmth and cold, hunger or not,
unbothered by word or thought,
a state of being sought by students of mindfulness,
full bellies inside warm houses.

Feeding the Birds in a Blizzard

Stranded in my house by the storm,
feeding oak and elm logs to the wood stove,
I feel secure as smoke rises from my chimney
and the chimneys of my rural neighbors.
Yet I worry about the pheasants
burrowing into snowdrifts for warmth,
the little chickadees and finches,
feathers flustered by the wind,
seeking shelter in woodpecker holes in dead trees,
the single robin doing the best it can,
competing with a gang of grackles
for the few crabapples left on the tree in my yard.

I worry about the people with nowhere to go
for shelter in this storm,
no one who cares enough to feed them.
Where will they go tonight,
with not even a stand of pine trees
to keep the wind at bay
and the storm predicted to intensify
when the dim light leaves the gray sky?

It would be foolish to drive into town in this weather,
the roads, drifted and unplowed,
impractical to gather the unsheltered from the sidewalks,
bring them home, offer them soup and a blanket,
a chair beside the fire in my hearth as the gospel bids us.
The best I can do today is the best I can do,
remember god is said to keep an eye on the sparrow, too,
so I shovel out the feeders again, refill them with seeds,
scatter corn on the snow like prayers
prayed for everything, myself included.

In the Eye of a Crow

Who could know?
The entirety of eternity
the formulation of creation
reflected in the eye of a crow.

I entreat you,
oh, raucous goddess,
forever feathered in ink,
do not blink.

A Cacophony of Crows

flies up from the carcass
at my approach.
With a stick, I prod the beaver's body,
its open, swollen belly already crawling.
Atop a naked elm, crows spread their wings,
yell at me to leave.
Returning a few days later,
I find a deflated body
already being inhaled by the soil,
fur blown away like milkweed silk.
The few bones not carried away by fox
are etched by the gnawings of field mice;
only the beaver's tail remains,
tough and unpalatable,
still as a poet's tongue
the morning after slapping water half the night
with poems of the inevitable.

I shrug my shoulders, turn to walk home,
talking to myself all the way.
None the wiser about life,
but more intent on living,
I watch for crows.

Congress

There's a crow convention
atop the tamarack trees,
a caucus—
everybody cawin'
everybody cussin'
nobody listenin',
a cacophonous congress of crows
that can't agree on anything;
which is probably best,
knowing what a mess of things,
how much shit
a flock of crows can dispense
if all of one mind.

Two Ravens

circle each other
in flight,
one carries a burning ember
in its beak,
the other,
a blue-and-green marble.
Far, far away
a flock of ravens so large
the sky is black
with feathers,
carry diamonds
in their beaks.
You can see the diamonds
but not the ravens,
not even the raven
carrying the marble
where you live.

Ravens in a Cottonwood Tree

speak a language of their own,
a patois of iridescent feathers
carried away by wind,
a dialect older than the tongue of the Navajo,
older than the words spoken
by the people who left the Great Rift Valley,
walked around the world naming everything,
a language we understood
before becoming so self-important
and replaced words with noise.
We don't remember the old tongues,
don't know what the wind says anymore
as it speaks in the trees,
what rock and water say to us.
Poetry comes close, music even closer,
the language of listening closest of all,
though it's all gibberish, meaningless
to the ravens in the cottonwood tree
who have to outshout us
just to have a conversation about bread crumbs.

Vultures

We flock
to carcasses
lying along the roadside.
We call ourselves poets.
We call
this shredding of flesh,
this tearing of guts,
this pecking of eyeballs
poetry.

When a Jenny Wren

or a tiny yellow warbler
mistaking the reflection of trees
in your window
for a passage through the woods,
hits the glass with a terrible thud,
like a dying heart's final beat,
rush out your door,
gently cup the dazed little flyer
in your warm hands,
whisper words of comfort,
tell the quivering little singer
how beautiful it is,
how honored you feel in its presence,
how sorry you are it was deceived
by a reflection in your house's windows.
Remind the little bird we are all fooled
by images of ourselves.
Hold the bird in your hands awhile,
hold it in your heart forever.
When the light returns to its eyes,
release it with a blessing,
the way a song is released
from the strings of a strummed guitar.

Nighthawks

Who can count nighthawks in flight?
Swooping, diving, soaring,
swerving between aspens and tamaracks,
skimming over a field of unmown grass
with just a tilt of wing, turn of tail,
feeding on insects invisible to me—
there must be thirty, if there are three.
This sky dance, this circling, criss-crossing,
infinitely intricate ballet of flight
seems choreographed to a man and his wife,
both bound by life and death to earth,
but whose spirits somehow soar
while watching feasting nighthawks fly
as sunset paints a rose and purple sky.

A Scarlet Tanager

flutters to the ground
from a dead willow branch
like a drop of blood falling
from the cross of Jesus.
Though there is no sin involved,
and certainly no religion,
there is some kind of redemption,
salvation in this vision,
for eyes burned by the glare
of too many tv screens,
computer monitors,
too many neon lights,
the reflections of too many headlights
on too many highways.

Shrike

At sunset, a foolish, hungry vole
emerges from a tunnel in the snow,
intent only on filling its cheeks
with seeds kicked from the bird feeder
by rambunctious nuthatches.
Careless, no thought of the shrike
that strikes from an aspen branch,
silently and swift,
the unwary little vole
is carried away in the grip of sharp talons,
still twitching as the shrike impales it
on a fence barb
before opening the vole's gray coat.

Three Sandhill Cranes

My eyes are blessed
with the grace in flight
of three sandhill cranes,
silhouetted black on gray
against the bulging water skins
of rain clouds yet to burst.

The part of me that flies
takes wing.
I forget my feet of clay,
realize the words I say,
no matter how articulate,
are the same cry
as cranes in flight,
repeated over and again.

I am here I am here I am here

one small chickadee

one small chickadee
alights on snow-covered branch
spawns a crystal squall

you know, of course
you are the chickadee in this poem
you fly through your little life

helpless but to do what you do
forever searching for another minute
to gleam in your dark eyes

Small

The sun rises as the moon sets.
A great horned owl hoots in the distance,
I hear wild turkeys gobble and chuckle
in the oak woods down the road.
Above, migrating snow geese honk,
wood ducks whistle, cranes yodel,
a cardinal sings desperately for love
and my neighbor's rooster
announces another day,
another large day,
and I, surrounded by this moment,
am small.

Bluebird on the Roof

An early bluebird alights
on the roof peak outside my window,
dances a little hop-step dance,
cocks his head side to side
in rhythm with the happy blues,
the fills and trills
I whistle through my harmonica,
maybe feeling he's got a song coming
from one of these earth walkers
whom he's graced with song
for all his cerulean-feathered life.
I feel blessed when he looks me in the eye,
does one more little hop-step,
seems to give me a nod of his head
before flying off to a cottonwood tree,
the day's business at hand,
as I return the harp to my pocket,
step out the door to my own day's work
with a heart renewed.

III

White Privilege

On the radio, a story of food riots in Venezuela,
hungry crying babies, angry screaming mothers.
What can I do, unable to invite them to dinner?
In my hand, a book, a story of not so long ago,
helicopters raining bullets
from the sky above villages in Sudan,
babies bathed in blood,
mothers, their lives bleeding out into the sand,
daughters raped, sons beaten,
fathers led away, never to return,
their village burned to ashes.
And just last night in St. Paul,
Philando Castile killed in his car,
in front of his girlfriend and her small daughter,
stopped because a black man can be stopped anytime
for a busted taillight and everyone knows
black men get bullets, not fix-it tickets.
This, a couple days after Alton Sterling
was shot in Baton Rouge for selling CDs on the street.

All this on a day I'm taking pictures of swimming ducklings,
two spotted fawns nursing from their mother,
a day I'm practicing fingering frets on my guitar,
a day my smiling niece sends photos of her smiling son.
In my house, filled with food,
in my house where no one is bleeding or dead,
where no one is crying but me for myself,
powerless to make wrong right,
I sit at a computer writing poems,
a vulture feeding on corpses, cursing each and every god.
I know people have been killed on account of poetry,
though I don't fear that I will be.
This is white privilege.

To Be Taken Seriously as a Poet

Write, write, write, of course,
write poems of the down-trodden,
social injustice, environmental degradation,
write about your government
(any government will do)
killing children, bombing hospitals,
taking food from people's mouths,
driving them into the sea to drown.

Write about gulags, concentration camps,
prisons and jails filled by "dissidents,"
put the blame where it belongs.
Write about the treatment of black people,
brown and yellow, red and white people.
Then write about doing something about it.

To ensure your notoriety,
submit these poems of subversion (they say),
poems of truth (I say),
to the FBI, CIA, BIA, KGB, Homeland Security,
scream free verse at the Pentagon,
everywhere that people who make up "the truth"
don't want to hear about "truth."
Just ask Berrigan or Solzenitzin, Mandela,
ask Leonard Pelltier . . .
Make your life a poem that rings truth,
that witnesses truth with a shout.
Though truth remains a metaphor,
you will be recognized,
perhaps with your name on a blacklist,
perhaps with pepper spray, perhaps with manacles,
water cannons, nightsticks, rubber bullets,
real bullets entering your already bleeding heart.

A Toothache During the Bombing of Baghdad

The throbbing wisdom tooth kept me up three nights
with three days of pain between,
each throb followed by another heartbeat of hurt,
but that's all it was; just pain, plain old pain—
no misery, agony, anguish, or torment, just pain.
It was just a toothache that hurt like hell,
but I thought that there's probably some poor bastard
hiding in a bombed-out basement in Baghdad
whose wisdom tooth is throbbing just like mine
and he has no shot of blessed novocaine, no laughing gas,
no pretty nurses, lifting his shirt, fitting him with monitors
before they put him under for the extraction.
All that man has is prayer to ease his pain
and a gun that he's thinking about using on his tooth.
All he can manage is half-awake sleep
but no pretty nurse wakes him
after a while to tell him he can go home now,
his pain is gone.

Only in a Democracy

Only in a democracy
Do the fire hydrants
And car tires
Elect the dogs
That piss on them

Guns

Turning the pages of Sunday's paper,
eyes spilling tears upon reading
of the ambush killing of a local cop,
and elsewhere, cops as killers,
the horror of the murders
of twenty angels and their guardians
at a small-town school,
people just having a holiday party,
going to a movie,
people attending church, for god's sake.
I make my way to the sports section,
that fantasy land of touchdowns,
home runs and slam dunks,
only to find stories of drunken outfielders
and homicidal/suicidal linebackers
wielding pistols,
followed by a half-page ad
for the Guns and Gear store,
urging me to get in on the deals—
an assault rifle, only $649.99,
semi-automatic pistols from $319 to $549,
all the ammo a person could need
to shoot up a school, a theater, a mall, a business,
a synagogue or mosque or church,
even an army base.
My sorrow vinegars to frustration and anger,
that my letters to so-called representatives
must be written on thousand-dollar bills
to even get a reading,
answered by a staffer's reply that says nothing,
and, in the end, dear god,
I'm left with prayer and poetry,
the children of necessity, drowning in futility.

At the Holiday Craft Fair

Faced by two short flights of stairs
that may as well be a mountain
between a young woman
sitting in her electric wheelchair
and the bake sale sweets,
Christmas ornaments, earrings,
paintings, pottery, and poetry books
on the upper level of an old church,
she stares at the stairs, fidgets in her chair,
and from the look I see in her eyes,
I imagine she'd like to rev up that chair,
pop the clutch as if driving a low-rider
down the mean streets in some neon town,
leave a patch of smoking rubber a block long,
shoot a rooster tail of loose gravel in the faces
of the minions of inconsideration,
the thugs of thoughtlessness,
give the finger to fate in her rearview mirror,
stuck again on the ground floor
of another heartless day.

Doll

Eyes wide but lifeless,
unfocused,
she stares out the plastic window
of her sealed box house
like someone depressed,
glassy eyes watching a tv
that may or may not be turned on.

In her back is a key hole,
a mechanism to animate her
in some pseudo-human way,
to speak simple words of need,
shed tears of frustration and sadness
that she must depend on another
for what little life she has—
a toy taken out, then put away
at the whim of someone
who only wants to play, or worse,
merely place her on display.

At Recovery Plus

With the voice of a crow,
a tear in his eye,
an Anishinaabe man from the Red Lake Rez
read a poem by Jimmy Santiago Baca*
as if he'd lived this poem his whole life,
a poem of being someone, but having nothing,
nothing to give to those he loved but love.
Each time he read the words "I love you"
he spoke to everyone he held in his heart,
including the people in this room,
people "in recovery,"
his heart big enough to hold the entire world,
the way a poem can hold the world.
When the poem ended,
a hush like the time of night birds stop singing
came upon us all, each having "recovered"
just a little, for a short while, maybe forever.

*"I Am Offering This Poem"

Migration Variations

I

A flock of cedar waxwings
harvests crabapples
from a tree I call mine.
Good workers,
work 'til the work's done
then move on;
good workers,
I don't pay 'em shit
but I don't check green cards
and I keep the cat in the house.

II

After harvest
I drink 'til I'm blind,
then drive all night,
Dakota to Nebraska,
another field,
another farmer bitchin'.
Sunrise accelerates.
I stop at a roadside well
and the coldest drink of water
I've ever tasted.
I wet my handkerchief,
drape it over my neck,
close my eyes,
see myself from a distance.

I see a killdeer
acting broken-winged
in the face of a fox,
running in circles
that ripple farther and farther
from my nest.

III

Even if my body
continues to live in this little house,
I know the real me
living in this house of bone
is as surely a migrant
as the red-breasted nomads
resting in the crabapple tree,
barely keeping ahead of the first snow.
Unlike me, those robins know
where they're going and how to get there,
where to stop for frost-softened apples.
Each fall I feel winter's breath blow colder,
ruffling the feathers on my neck.
I have no idea where I'm going,
only know that I am moving
with no internal compass to guide me
and a need to find sustenance
every day of my journey.

Memorials of Plastic Flowers

faded to dull pastels
by sun and wind-blown sand,
mark places of accidental death,
the result of inattention, alcohol, speed
along two-lane highways in border states,
Texas, New Mexico, Arizona,
into Colorado and Kansas.
Like habitats and planting zones
trying to outrun a changing climate,
these memorials of make-believe flowers
have migrated north
like Mexican workers into Minnesota,
appearing after the snow melts.
Not surprising.
How fast would you drive
to get to a bar for some relief,
or home to your family,
a change of clothes, a shower, sleep,
after working the midnight shift
cutting the heads and feet off chickens
so someday your children
will not be strangers in this land,
be allowed to live with dignity,
not be buried alone beneath the snow?

Minnesota's No Different

Dakota soil migrates to Minnesota
in brown blizzards,
fills the low spots in the landscape
after the snow has melted away
like the brown blizzard of immigrants
fills the low places all over America.
Minnesota's no different.
Spanish is spoken by harvest crews
in the Red River valley,
Asian dialects ring on the killing floor
of the Cold Spring chicken processing plant;
not the kind of jobs
most parents want for their kids;
no future there for the grandchildren
of northern European immigrants
who've melted into the middle class,
the sons and daughters of Red River farmers
moving away to Minneapolis.

What Would She Think of Poetry

Where does the haggard mother
of six children, all fathered by rape,
bloated with starvation
in a dusty refugee camp
send her spirit for solace
when she's never known solace?

Can she even know sorrow
when she's known nothing but sorrow?

What does she feel when the red sun sets
in a cerulean sky,
when stars twinkle in an inky sea?

What would she think of poetry?

What would she think of me?

Is it only because my stomach is full,
my skin is white,
no one is shooting at me,
that I can write of beauty,
the flight of a hummingbird,
a bumblebee,
black-eyed susans or poetry?

That Ol' Cleanliness Is Next to Godliness Conundrum

An old gospel song
says His eye is on the sparrow
and, by implication, the fat robin
I watch taking a splash bath
in a shallow puddle
at the edge of an irrigated lawn.
I've been told His eye is on you and me,
clean as only Americans can be,
with all the water we want,
but no one seems to have his eye
on the Ethiopian women, backs bent low,
carrying water from a sporadic muddy seep
back to their village on a dry mountain,
fifty pounds, twenty miles, every single day,
hoping to keep their children alive
and their husbands happy one more day.
None of them has taken a bath in their lives,
but they seem at least as godly
as the whistle-clean people filling the pews beside me,
their thoughts already on an afternoon at the lake
as they bow their heads in prayer.

Disparity and Despair at Super America

I

While you're gassing up your old car,
carefully counting your change,
debating whether to buy a quarter tank or a half;
a pair of matching Harleys,
ostentatious in their growling,
pull up to the next pump,
their riders dressed in silver-studded leather
worth more than your entire wardrobe;
a couple out for a weekend spin
as you head to your second part-time job,
both of them, dead end.

II

You shake your head in befuddled despair
as a gas-hog SUV towing a sailboat
christened *Donald's Wet Dream*,
bigger than your fantasies,
drives up beside you,
a family heading north
to a mansion they call "the cabin,"
spending a hundred bucks on gas and doughnuts,
while your kids beg for a candy bar to split
and a paddle-boat ride in the city park pond.

III

There's a tricked-out pickup truck at the far pump
towing a trailer loaded with dirt bikes and jet skis,
some dude dressed in new camo, cap on backwards,
high-fiving his two kids dressed the same,
gassing up the truck and the big-boy toys,
just out to have a little weekend fun.
Your kids stare with full-moon eyes,
before going home to the old bike they share
on the busy city street that scares you,
but you just can't keep saying no to everything.

IV

A shiny red convertible
some daddy bought for his daughter's graduation
parks at the pump behind you,
full of giggling blonde girls,
all talking on cell phones,
laughing their way to the mall,
credit cards tucked into the pockets of hundred-dollar jeans
you hope to see at Goodwill next month for twenty bucks
and then you think
where in hell am I gonna get twenty bucks for jeans?

V

A motor home, big as your apartment,
plastered with bumper stickers from Yellowstone,
Yosemite, the Grand Canyon, and the Everglades,
satellite dish on the roof, bicycles on the bumper,
towing a small car behind
for getting away from the campground on day trips
to souvenir shops and restaurants in tourist towns,
casts a shadow over you, your car, your family inside.
A day trip to the county park on a small lake
is the only vacation your family will have,
an afternoon of cane-pole fishing from the public pier
with bobbers and worms you dug yourself
hoping you might catch enough fish for dinner.

Dreams

. . . and I bet
that if some corporation could find a way
to make you pay for your dreams, they would;
and, of course, the rich would get the best dreams,
the dreams with the hottest women
or the guys with chiseled abs, the coolest cars,
all the best adventures in dreamland,
and because the rule is you get what you pay for,
the poor get only cheap nightmares,
though they get to keep them on awakening,
while the rich wake to another daydream.

The Anniversary Gift

Yolanda picks the green ferns in the bouquet
you give your wife on your anniversary.
When she was younger,
Yolanda could pick 400 bundles a day,
but now her back is so sore from bending for hours,
a good day is less than half of that;
her hands are so swollen she can't work some days,
her fingers ache so that she can't sleep at night,
and that's not to mention the snakes
that sneak into the warm, humid fernery,
sprayed with the same chemicals sprayed on the ferns,
causing rashes on Yolanda's skin which never cease to itch.
She has no protective gear and no one cares.
Yolanda is replaceable.

But you love your wife. It's your anniversary.
You hope the bouquet you bring home after work
will be enough to keep your wife from replacing you,
though if either of you knew about Yolanda,
you might opt for chocolates and wine,
but what about Miguel and his family in the vineyards,
right here in California's wine country,
eating their lunch in the backwash of sprayed pesticides.
What about his back, his hands, his ragged breathing,
what they put themselves through so they all can eat.

What about Drissa, a child slave on the cacao plantation
in the Ivory Coast or Mombi Bakayoko in Mali,
children, kidnapped for slave labor at age seven,
the beatings and malnourishment that goes into chocolate
they've never even tasted and never will.

Better to wrap your wife in your arms so tightly
that she melts like chocolate in the sun of your embrace,
kiss her like you're newlyweds on honeymoon,
tell her that her lips taste like a fine cabernet.
Write her a poem with words like roses
grown in your own garden.

Diamonds

The ads and commercials
say a man in love
should prove his love with diamonds—
a big shiny rock for her finger,
bright bangles to dangle from her ears,
diamonds to pin to her nose, lip, navel,
hang from her neck to accent her breasts.
But not my woman; she would never wear
the misery of Africa on her ring finger,
hang the cries of child labor from her ears,
pin the slaughter of silver-backed gorillas
anywhere on her beautiful body;
she'd never hang pain, destruction, or injustice
between her life-giving breasts.

Domatila's Husband*

I am not stupid, nor am I a fool.
I may be stubborn and weak,
but I am not hard-hearted.
I am a man
who has learned to be honest with himself.

The breath in my lungs
wheezes that truth is truth,
no matter if spoken by woman or man.
My aching back screams about truth.
Pain does not lie,
but pain can close your eyes.

So you see, I am not blind,
though blinded
by the darkness of old ways
handed down to me from my father,
blinded by the false light
of a lying general's broken promises.

Woman, I have ears that hear,
I have eyes that see.
I am a man with a heart that cries
from deep in a mine for daylight.
Woman, lead me to the sun.

*After reading *Let Me Speak!* by Domitila
Barrios de Chungara

Clay

Hypnotized by the spinning wheel,
obsessed with mud, the potter
shapes bowls of clay
day after day after day;
so many bowls,
they push each other
off the crowded shelf.
Shards mound like a new grave,
leaving no room for buttercups,
pitcher plants or plated armadillos.
The potter does not rest
though there is not enough
cereal or milk to fill each bowl,
even if divided equally.

IV

Advice for a Road Trip
for Maluszcka

Use your turn signals, damn it.
Keep your speed close to the limit.
Use your side mirrors.
Come to a full stop at stop signs.
Pull over and sleep when you're tired.

You've got a map;
you know how to follow the red highways
between here and there.
You know where you want to go;
but all those other fools on the road
don't have a clue,
may not even see you.
Just use your turn signals, damn it.

That's enough advice; you know the rest—
how to light up your eyes when you laugh,
how to keep an open mind,
open hands,
an open heart.
Be honest with yourself.
Use your turn signals, damn it.

Irene, South Dakota

You drive down into another fold of South Dakota,
find Irene,
a little town in a low place,
a mirage on the prairie,
some old houses, a church, a few closed-up stores,
a grain mill, a gas station.
You don't need gas, so you don't stop.
You climb back out of the valley,
say good night to Irene in your rearview mirror,
swallowed by a wrinkle in the Great Plains
you're skittering across,
mindless as a bug on a rumpled blanket.

Another Starry Night

Ever since God invented iPods
and deigned that I should have one,
my criteria for downloading a song
is how it's gonna sound at one or two a.m.
on a two-lane highway
outside of Shallow Water, Kansas,
when everyone in the van is asleep
and the stars are swirling
as if the sky is a van Gogh painting.

Approaching Sharon Springs

Driving through Kansas at two a.m.,
everyone in the van asleep but me,
hands on the steering wheel, eyes on the road,
and the Grateful Dead, jamming "Dark Star,"
time and space becoming irrelevant.
Across the expanse of the Great Plains,
Sharon Springs is just another minor sun
called a star after dark by the inhabitants
of a trivial planet of rock,
lonely as a cork floating in the sea,
despite the illusion we've chosen to embrace
in order to make sense of our being
in this particular anywhere, anywhen;
of being at all.

The God of Dumb Luck

Only an old fool from Minnesota,
because winter hasn't killed him
after sixty-seven attempts,
and because he's fueled by a vision of spring
in the high desert of New Mexico—
mesas and buttes baked by a sun
exuding heat as well as light,
so unlike the winter sun of the north,
would chance driving in this snowstorm
on icy U.S. 27
south of Sharon Springs, Kansas,
trying to reach La Junta, Colorado, by midnight
and Abiquiu, New Mexico, Ghost Ranch by lunch.
But, here I am,
hands gripping the steering wheel so tightly
my fingers have locked up,
leaning into the windshield
in hope of spotting a line on the highway
to guide me on this fool's errand.
To turn back would be even more half-witted,
so I drive on into the storm, fool that I am,
praying to the God of Dumb Luck
for a snow plow's spinning beacon to appear.

Between La Jara and Romeo

van Gogh wakes in the back seat,
looks out the window,
asks me if I could stop the universe,
it being so difficult to paint spinning objects.
I say no and Vincent begins to cry,
waking Picasso in the passenger seat,
who also looks out and wonders aloud
why the mesquite bushes look like mandolins
with broken strings and bloated bodies.
Georgia O'Keefe speaks from the radio,
asks if we could backtrack a mile,
she says she saw some cattle skulls
she could use in a painting.
I shake my head, say no to the radio,
no one can go back, only forward,
though Pablo thinks sideways is a possibility.
Vincent's gone back to sleep holding his ear
as we pull into Manassa to pick up Jack Dempsey,
in need of someone to keep order in this poem.

In Tierra Amarilla

Intensely significant
for who and what it is,
an old black dog,
muzzle white
as an *abuelo*'s beard,
eyes clouded with age,
lazes on a sunny step
outside a blue door
hung on rusty hinges
set in an adobe wall
in Tierra Amarilla.
I'm lying in the sun
with that old black dog,
though you can't see me
in this photo,
for that, and anything else you
might see in these words
you need poetry.

One Afternoon in Santa Fe

October.
Santa Fe.
Los álamos, dorados,
el cielo, azul,
pozole at La Choza,
and you, *mi amor, feliz,*
sitting across the table from me.

After lunch, we tour
the Museum of Indian Arts and Culture;
my eyes fill like rain clouds
building above the Sangre de Cristos
at what I see in the exhibit,
tears born of beauty as well as cruelty,
how each is born from the other,
though I suspect these people of the past,
their lives made of clay and blood,
the same as is my life,
would laugh at tears cried on their account,
would tell me to save my tears for my own sorrows,
live this day made of *pozole*
at busy little La Choza,
los álamos, dorados,
el cielo, azul,
and you, *mi amor, feliz,*
sitting across the table from me.

One Evening in Santa Fe

Windows darken around the Plaza.
Turquoise and silver vendors,
wood carvers and chili pepper merchants,
leather workers and weavers
close up shop as the sky purples and blushes.
A solo trumpeter blows his horn from the bandshell,
on his knees as if offering a prayer,
then leaning against the wall like a casual smoker
in a 1940s black-and-white B movie,
sending his music, plaintive and poignant,
into the rarified ether of Santa Fe
while *turistas*, foot-weary, over-stimulated and overspent
sip twenty-dollar glasses of Bordeaux
on the balconies and verandas of chic restaurants,
paying no attention to the music filling the air,
though it would expand inside their hearts,
a gift of bittersweet melancholy,
if they would allow it entrance.
No money floats down to the trumpeter's upturned fedora,
as if his music provides mere ambiance,
not the song that the holiness of each moment sings.
It seems poets are the only people who cry
when a trumpet blows blue notes at gloaming.

Near the Harbor in Victoria

I could find a dozen reasons
to walk by the beggar and his dog,
all of them cliché—
he'll just buy booze
or that "teach a man to fish" platitude,
meaningless if you're hungry now,
have no money to buy a license
or a place to cook a fish, anyhow.

I buy the beggar a sandwich,
some meat for his mutt,
sit on the sidewalk, talk awhile,
scratch the dog's ears, rub her belly,
before we all slip back into our lives,
but imagining myself and my dog
on some cold sidewalk somewhere,
Mojo howling the blues
as I play an old harmonica
and cigar box guitar,
hoping to attract tourists with fat wallets,
a sandwich, a little conversation.

Little Minnesota Town

The bars and pizza joints keep Main Street busy after dark;
the church does the same on Sunday morning,
but the daytime stores have mostly died,
migrated toward the four-lane commuter's highway
or been reinvented and renovated once again.
The bank and meat market have gone around the corner,
the bank, now a recording studio.
A town founder's family grocery has become housing,
the Chevy dealership, torn down and snow-fenced.
The used book store/Mexican restaurant/kitchen supply store
is vacant, for rent again, its one empty black eye
reflects the traffic of cars on the way to church,
but mostly an empty parking lot.

Over on the four-lane you can buy gas and bait
and visit the beauty parlor, all in the same pole building.
You've got your choice of two liquor stores,
each sporting inflatable beer cans
anchored to cement blocks in their parking lots.
On the highway strip
there is a café and a couple convenience stores,
each with twenty gas pumps, standing surreally
beneath buzzing neon flourescence and muzak.
Along the highway you can wash your car or repair its body,
buy a snowblower or lawnmower or some plumbing putty.
On Main Street a new beautification project has been finished,
but the parking spaces fill only for funerals.

St. Joseph Post Office, 9:00 a.m.

An old man enters the St. Joseph Post Office;
the town's widows chatting in the lobby
after morning Mass fall into a mutual silence,
then resume their gossip when he leaves,
a couple white envelopes and some fliers
clutched in his arthritic hand.
They all know his wife, waiting in the car,
fixing her hair in the rearview mirror,
seemingly not noticing them chatting in the lobby.
She shuffles through the mail
as her husband checks his mirrors for cars,
before driving off to more errands.
The widows keep chatting but they all watch the car turn the corner,
shaking their heads as they talk,
before going home, catalogs and magazines in hand,
if lucky, a letter or card from a grandchild
that puts a smile on a widow's face
that lasts the day long,
along with certain bragging rights, for a day, anyway,
among the other grandmothers,
before they all return to spotless spouseless houses
to reread the day's mail at the kitchen table.

If We Make It to Willmar

A crosswind laced with snow and South Dakota soil
gains strength as it races across miles of empty Minnesota fields,
rocks our little car as we drive out of the Redwood River valley
on black-ice backroads and slushy ruts that steal the wheels.
Alone in the car, we don't say much,
intent as animals on the weather, senses sharpened.
While "Asleep at the Wheel" sings from an electronic Somewhere
about miles and miles of sunny Texas,
my hands white-knuckle the steering wheel,
shoulders ache from fighting the wind for control of the car
as we drive past half a dozen others nose down in the ditch.
If we can make it to Willmar, I think, we'll be okay;
the prairie gives way to sheltering elms and oaks and maples there,
the highway will be dry and the wind broken
if we can only make it to Willmar.

A Walk on the Lake Wobegon Trail

Early on an April morning,
I set out from the trail terminal in St. Joseph.
As I settle into my stride, I daydream
the sun rising behind me
is the headlight of an old locomotive
steaming over the eastern horizon,
loaded with boxcars full of new days;
dropping off one for each person in town,
before continuing west to Avon and Albany
and all the other little towns
on the edge of the waking prairie,
almost able to feel the vibrations
of squealing, sparking steel wheels
come up through my feet.
Suddenly a great horned owl hoots
like a far-off train whistle,
bringing me back from my reverie—
a side trip on a side track
inside this longer journey we're all taking.

Pretty Stones Below Sleeping Bear Dune

Walking the beach below the Sleeping Bear,
looking for pretty stones, interesting rocks,
carried here by a glacier ten thousand years ago,
polished by the water of what people,
not knowing the name the lake calls itself,
named Lake Michigan.
I lose myself in the song of breaking waves,
each wave introducing itself,
before returning home without leaving home.
So intent on finding the miracle in each stone
lying half-buried in sugar sand
or on display in the shop window of the lake,
I forget my own name,
forget that I need to keep breathing,
forget my heart needs to keep pumping blood,
forget that I have a body at all,
though some entity must be leaving these footprints
in the sand behind me.

Pleasant Acres

These acres are not ecstatic
nor scream-your-lungs-out
orgasmic rapturous.
These are not blissful acres,
felicitous, enchanting, or beguiling,
though they may have been
back when deer and antelope played here.
Nor, on the other hand,
are these acres painful or afflicted,
blighted or unsightly scenes of ruin.
Pleasant.
These acres are nice enough;
a bit bland, perhaps, and not unique—
houses all much the same as each other
and most any other house anywhere,
painted in washed-out colors,
surrounded by predictable lawns;
a place to park your car at night
while you eat microwaved food, watch tv.
These acres are nice, okay, all right;
pleasant.

Boulder Crossing

A name to evoke . . . what,
Boulder, Colorado—
a view of snow-capped mountains
suddenly bloomed in a subdivision
upon a pancake-flat sand plain
in central Minnesota?

Or just big-ass rocks
suddenly popped out of a former cornfield
needing to be crossed by four-wheel-drive truck
just to get to your half-million-dollar
"one-third-acre estate with all the amenities,"
three-car garage, sunroom, mudroom,
bedroom with private bath and hot tub,
walk-in closets and pantry,
kitchen fit for a French chef,
though you microwave most of your meals.

Perhaps the name is a warning,
like cattle crossing or deer crossing,
except that you need to be wary of boulders
randomly rolling across paved cul-de-sacs.
It seems you've got to be rugged,
a real pioneer opening new lands
to settle in Boulder Crossing.

The Wilds

The old farm houses along gravel roads
have been bought up, torn down,
sold when the kids decided on college degrees
instead of milking cows,
when corn and soybeans and alfalfa
could no longer pay the taxes.
The pavers and developers moved in,
moved out beaver and muskrat lodges
in favor of bi-levels and colonials—
not called houses, but "home packages"
costing 250 thou up to a mill.
In this new place, called "The Wilds,"
landscaped lawns have replaced gamma grass
where field mice and voles once tunneled,
hidden from the great horned owl's gaze.
Woodchuck and raccoon dens have been bulldozed
for tennis courts and a golf course;
ponds drained, replaced by pools and splash pads.
The old elms, riddled by woodpeckers,
where oriole nests hung like ornaments,
have been chain-sawed, given way to ornamentals.
The Wilds, electrically lighted at night,
hides the Pleiades in a luminescent haze
born from fear of people preying on other people.
Welcome to The Wilds—country comfort, city ease.

V

Connection

People still call the place the rabbit farm, though it's been years since old man Chance raised rabbits here. The college bought the property, bulldozed the old house and all the rabbit hutches, funny little buildings, one painted red, another yellow, some sided with brown or green shingles, all capped with roofs of different pitches, some pointed, some flat, one rounded, and all filled with rows of wire mesh cages housing New Zealand Whites, Flemish Giants, or Californians.

Mrs. Chance grew flowers all over the rabbit farm's yard. She had a large garden, an orchard of apple and plum trees, beds of gladiolus and tiger lilies and a hedge of honeysuckle. She kept it all immaculately free of weeds; you could drive by the place any summer day and most likely, you'd see her on her knees beside a flower bed scratching out weeds with a silver-handled three-fingered claw.

One day while weeding, the phone must have rung or maybe some of the rabbits got loose, so Mrs. Chance rose from her garden and placed her hoe in a hole in the old elm north of the house, and for some reason, forgot about it. Old Mrs. Chance died without ever remembering, the elm grew tall, surrounded her claw with decades of tree rings before Dutch elm disease claimed the old tree, which brings my story to 1993, September 23rd, exactly, and a man cutting firewood years after Mrs. Chance forgot her hoe.

There were sparks and smoke when the screaming chainsaw cut through the hoe's aluminum handle, but nothing like the lightning that illuminated the space between life and death for an instant, long enough to show the woodcutter that the past hovers all around us, how even strangers' lives connect in the heartwood of old trees.

Raffle

The parish widows, scrap savers,
scrapbook makers, wrinkle-fingered
quilters of salvaged cotton and wool,
like collectors of snake skins,
gather the shed clothing
of growing or shrinking people,
patch their stories together,
while sewing Sunday shirts to curtains,
baby clothes to grandmas' dresses. Quilts
sewn by Christian hands, warmth and security
you can pull over your head at night—
two dollars a chance, three for five dollars.

Noon

Grandpa rocks back and forth on the porch,
so slowly he seems asleep,
lulled by the purr of his son's diesel tractor
idling in the turnaround
beneath a broken old box elder
that once shaded the horses
as they rested and drank after plowing.
Where the horses once slopped,
a thick patch of green grass
ringed the wooden trough;
now there stands a fuel barrel,
weeds splashed black beneath a leaky spigot.
Grandpa appears to be still dozing,
though he's out somewhere walking through his life.

Potato Farm

The harvest crew sprawls on the lawn,
while the potato digger and trucks
idle in the turnaround
like horses in the shade.
We lie beneath tall elms, resting,
our bellies full of home-grown Angus
and all the potatoes we could eat.

Grandpa Hartmann comes out of his house
with an old photo from back in the thirties.
It's a picture of another harvest crew,
lying beneath scrawny elm seedlings,
holes in their pants' knees, shaggy-haired;
they look a lot like we do.
He said at noon they told stories and smoked,
horsed around, just like we do.
He says things haven't really changed much;
they worked like all hell, same as we do.
Work's still the only way he knows
to get something to eat, he said.

A Song, Himself
for Mike Raymond

Those songs he sang,
full of life,
full of love for the least among us,
for the world he loved;
the chords he strummed,
the notes he picked,
have been set free to wander the ether
as he's been set free from his burden.
His songs settle where they may,
perhaps to be heard once more
by ears we can't imagine,
while someone else strums his guitar.
A song himself, he's gone
the way a song fades away on the radio,
yet he settles sweetly in our memories
like a song we'll never forget.

Laddie

The widow cinches the saddle of her dead husband's horse,
a gentle gelding from a line of Missouri Foxtrotters and Zane Greys,
on a summer Sunday morning, mosquitos humming,
the smell of campfire smoke in the air.
She wonders if its equine mind
is picturing her old man stepping into the stirrup,
hand on the saddlehorn,
swinging his leg over the cantle,
the familiar weight of his body in the saddle instead of hers,
remembering the way his hands worked the reins,
rather than the way her hands guide him
on this wooded path, up and down these hills.
She wonders if the white gelding feels him riding with her
on this bittersweet trail through the woods,
as surely astride his horse's back as she is,
hand patting its neck, fingers entwined in its mane,
voice in its ears, singing some old cowboy song.
Whoopi-tai-yai-yo,
Oh, Laddie-o.
Oh, Laddie, Laddie,
Oh, Laddie-o.

My Old Friend, Jack

Wears worn-down boots
laced with broken laces, hanging untied,
torn jeans and a ragged jacket;
his hair hangs uncombed, as usual,
greasy tangles dangle from beneath a dirty cap;
his calloused hands, nicked up, scabbed over
like you'd expect a working man's hands to look,
grab my hand when I remove my mitten.
Jack's face has grown wrinkled as elm skin,
his eyes shine from behind smoke-squinting crow's feet,
half confused; but you know he's not—
Jack knows what's going on,
just finds it all so ironic,
but his eyes are full of mischief and wonder
at whatever the moment holds out to him.
Jack acts like it's something everyone would know
if they just paid attention to anything at all
and will figure it out for themselves eventually.

Two Different Boots

We never knew his real name.
He just showed up on the farm
one morning during potato harvest
looking for work, but he was gone
by morning coffee break.
We called him Billy Odd Boots,
still do when we tell his story.
Billy Odd Boots wore one black boot,
an old combat boot, on his right foot.
On his left, a beat-up brown work boot,
laced with two white laces, tied together,
a worn-down heel that made it seem as if Billy limped.

Billy Odd Boots' job that day
was loading a semi-trailer
with hundred-pound bags of russets and reds,
stacked crosswise, five high. And in between times
Billy had to carry the bags of bad spuds to the spreader.
It wasn't long, Billy was dragging those bags.
We could see that those hundred-pounders
were a match for Billy, and Billy could see it, too,
because after Billy dragged that third bag to the spreader,
he didn't come back.

We all stood in the door of the potato shed
and watched Billy Odd Boots running down the lane.
Black boot, brown boot, black boot, brown boot,
each goading the other like they were new tennies.
Billy flew, hardly kicking up a stone, and the last time we saw him
he was hitchhiking towards town.

Whatever lesson there may be in the story of Billy Odd Boots,
I'm sure it's just some sideways kind of moral.
Billy Odd Boots showed us it's easy to be free,
all you got to do is run, man. Run away.
I'd like to think that I'm as free as Billy Odd Boots,
that if something doesn't suit me, I can leave it like a footprint;
but being honest with myself, I see Billy was a running shoe,
and my foot's trapped in a work boot, nailed to the workshop floor.

Sheep

When winter settles in St. Joseph
Salvatore thickens with woolen layers;
long johns and wool socks,
a scratchy inner fleece
beneath a shaggy sweater, suspendered pants.
He adds a plaid cap with ear flaps down,
sheepskin mittens and a dirty brown coat.

Each morning, Salvatore waddles away
from early Mass at the shepherd's stable,
a glow on his wind-reddened face.
Footprints follow him through the snow;
he leaves them, frozen, outside his door.
Swallowed by his winter-dark house,
Salvatore awaits the wolf with coffee cup in hand.

A Little Smile

Outside Kay's Kitchen on a warm spring night,
a college boy and a college girl
on break from washing dishes and waiting tables,
talk about tests and term papers,
about being in debt up to their asses,
though only sophomores.
They see some friends walking in a group
down College Avenue toward Sal's and The La,
holler at them to save some beer for them.
Across the street the moon rises
over the Holiday store's neon sign.
They're not sure if it's the moon or the sign
blinking "gas, milk, cigs" shining in each others' eyes.
They both notice the moonlight, but say nothing.
He holds the door open for her,
she gives him a little smile, her eyes still lit.
Kay notices this and smiles to herself,
thinks about Dirk as a young man way back when.

Plan B

So this god
decided to open a nice resort
in a great location,
place called Eden,
but the customer base
just wasn't there,
nobody around
but this guy made of mud,
though he did have ribs,
one too many, I guess,
so this god
in an effort to get more clientele,
took the mud man's extra rib
and made it into a woman.
It seemed like the way to go,
until this woman, who favored apples,
ate one, shiny and red,
served to her by a serpent,
and because she ate this apple
she figured out lots of stuff
that God was going to keep secret
for her and mud man's own good.
But God, being God, said, hmmm,
this ain't workin',
so he went to Plan B,
in which the rest of us,
skin wrinkled as fallen fruit
were made to enter the world
through a vaginal tunnel, crying,
with a taste for apples.

The Mud People

And so, this god chooses a planet,
which the mud people call Earth,
out of all the mega-zillion planets
in this universe and all the other universes,
scoops up some mud from this planet
and shapes a couple mud people,
breathes on them,
kind of like mouth-to-mouth resuscitation,
and right away, they start walkin' and talkin',
already knowing the same language as God
and so they start talkin' to him,
talk about all kinds of stuff,
but God doesn't tell them much of anything, really,
and the mud people don't tell God everything, either.
But it was all copacetic until this snake shows up.
This snake able to speak the speak of the mud people,
tells them some of the stuff God didn't,
but some stuff, he just made up to suit himself,
and though it made sense to some of the mud people,
to others, it was just plain sinful,
and dude, that caused big problems.
Most of the mud people didn't know who to believe
and they still don't, their brains, after all, made of mud.

Eve

She's no supermarket apple,
waxed and polished
to look good under fluorescent light,
bruises and flaws hidden; tasteless
as photoshopped women in the tabloids
at the end of the check-out line.
She's a freckled, dimpled country girl,
naturally pretty in sunlight
like an apple on a backyard tree,
sweet, but a bit tart at the same time,
an apple that holds the knowledge
of good and evil and vacillates between,
delicious and tempting,
the offering of a serpent with good intentions,
the apple of its gleaming eye.

What Is Here Now

We climbed out of the Great Rift,
(an ironic a place name as ever there was),
though at the time it was only known as HERE.
We walked out of Africa, likewise only known as HERE,
circled the globe of earth, not knowing it was round,
and the only name earth had then was HERE.
We named everything in our path
with grunts and whistles and clicks of our tongues,
it seeming like the thing to do
so we didn't have to talk only with our eyes and hands anymore,
and it seemed to work out all right
until we began to name each other
instead of calling ourselves WE,
until inventing the name I for ourselves,
but where we really got ourselves into trouble
was when we invented the name GOD
for what had always been known as WHAT IS.
This led to the greatest of rifts;
we separated ourselves from the divine.
We disconnected ourselves from WHAT IS.
We don't know who we are anymore,
don't know the only time we have is NOW
or that NOW lasts forever, no matter the HERE.

Reader

He writes words
that aren't yet poems;
she strings beads
that aren't yet necklaces,
says let's make love later.
And he'd love to love her after reading
that steamy Brazilian novel by Amado.
In his lust
he wants to be Emiliano Guedes
on page 299;
she could be Tereza Batista.
He hopes he doesn't die in her arms,
but accepts this idea as possible;
though, after reading the last page,
he'd rather be Januario Gereba
returning from the sea,
she, of course, remaining Tereza.

Cyclops

If Cyclops was a Byclops,
had two gentle blue eyes,
binocular,
instead of one jaundiced yellow eye,
monocular,
he'd have sharper depth perception,
he'd be a better dancer,
at a wedding dance or hoedown,
find a more graceful groove,
bust a better move,
lighten up his footprint,
dance a dance balletic,
rather than a stomp, pathetic.
Having two blue eyes
might elevate a cyclops' mood,
tame the hornets in his head,
calm the cyclopean temper,
inherent since the time of Homer,
writing of brave Odysseus,
who, so eloquently reported
that he'd never met a cyclops
that in a kindly way comported.

While Reading Ferlinghetti

A rainy December afternoon;
while waiting for my computer to load
I'm reading Ferlinghetti,
"Matisse at the Modern, Magritte at the Met,"
a long poem inside a large book
populated with art and artists,
Communists and communists, dancers,
lovers of art, lovers of love, lovers of each other,
a boy, a bicycle, a barrel, a wheelchair,
nude women.
On the computer screen a message appears; I'm rudely distracted
by a woman who wants to connect with me, though only virtually,
so I close the book, mark the page, click the mouse,
say Sorry Lawrence, could you hold a minute,
I'm a lusty old goat living a fantasy life,
I'm sure you'll understand,
I'll get back to you as soon as I can.
But I find this woman wants only acknowledgment,
not a physical connection,
so I put away my fantasy erection, turn back to the poem,
resulting in a mental orgasm when I read of a Matisse nude,
one hand on her nipple, the other on her vulva.
The computer screen goes black and blank
but the poem glows red with heat. It's where I want to be.
I apologize to the poet. Lawrence, forgive me.
Can I meet you at the Modern, Fifty-third Street in Manhattan,
unless, of course, you've got to catch a flight of fantasy, yourself.

Where Is Ed Abbey's Grave?

First off,
I ain't about to die in a hospital bed.
Help me get these needles out of my arms
and get me the hell outta here;
no damn gravestone for me, either,
no name, no meaningless dates.
Drink some beer, put me in the ground
up on top of some mesa with a view
where my bones'll never be found.
If you must look for me,
look in a slinking coyote's eyes
or a cactus spine stuck on your boot,
the proverbial bur in your saddle.
I'll be the grit in your eyes and nose
when the wind blows sand,
the ripples in a stream
that's bone dry most of the year.
You might remember me with a curse
and a story,
remember when that goddamn Ed . . .
That said, I wouldn't care
if you sang a song of me,
as long as you only sang it once,
then let it fade into the ether
or buried it with my bones.
Just leave me the hell alone.

A Previously Owned Book*

Her name inscribed inside the cover,
the last person to read this book
is dead.
I know this because I knew her.
It was cancer that killed her,
not the book,
though the story on its pages
could tear apart any sensitive heart,
set it racing,
then stop it dead.

The Weight of All Things by Sandra Benitez
Inscribed: "To Nancy—Paz"

On the Occasion of the Visiting Guatemalan Poet, Danielle Makes Burritos for Thirty

Emilio,
a Guatemalan poet with thick black hair,
long as a winter night,
eyes reminding me of a raven's eyes,
a voice gentle as rain dripping from trees,
reads poems in Maya K'iche',
Español and English,
poems honoring the history and ancestry of his people,
poems of struggle and loss, triumph of spirit as well,
words that shrink the world for the listener.
When he finishes reading, the room is silent as soil,
holding the roots of the world,
wide as the sky that holds the sun.

After the reading, Danielle gives the call for dinner,
burritos made with rice, beans, squash, onions,
tomatoes, chilis, lettuce, and cheese,
salsas and guacamole, fresh as morning air,
all grown by water, sun, and soil,
worked by local farmers
who have, themselves, sprouted from the land.

As Danielle fills our plates, overfilling them,
her face glows red as an apple on the tree,
flushed with the heat of the kitchen,
eyes shining like sunlight on blue water,
her smile filled with a love and joy
that can only come from feeding others,
feeding not only stomachs, but souls as well,
each ingredient a word in a poem of her making
that can't be heard or spoken,
satisfying the part of us that hungers for life lived well.

Voyager Leaves Our Solar System

We will be dust in a rusted world
swallowed by an expanded sun,
as will be pyramids and pentagons,
popes and presidents, afterthoughts
of a dead planet, slowly spinning
without wind, water, or tongue,
though I am comforted, knowing
that pinballing between the stars
Voyager continues sailing on,
a cosmic jukebox
playing Johnny B. Goode,
Chuck Berry rockin' on
for any lifeform with the right coin,
some rock in its socks, some roll
in its extraterrestrial soul.

Cosmic Bread Recipe

In a bowl
that might be any shape,
or every shape,
or shapeless,
combine the mother of all bangs,
a big bang, a ginormous, gigonzo
BANG
that generates universes and galaxies,
suns and planets and moons,
comets and asteroids and dark matter,
and for that matter, time and space.
In this bowl mix in
gravity, geology, biology, hydrology, chemistry,
morph them into soil and water
and atmospheres.
Call some of this biology wheat,
some, honey, some, yeast,
call some of this geology salt;
chemistry, call it water.
Sculpt some of this biology into the shape of hands
to mix the above ologies together into dough;
knead it, pound it, caress it, shape it
into loaves of any shape or every shape or no shape,
bake this dough with heat of the above mentioned
BANG
and then eat it.
Know you are eating light,
that you are light.
Rejoice.

See What Happens

We're all the same.
We sail through the good times
like a pitcher throwing seven innings
of perfect baseball;
every fastball nips the corner of the plate,
every curve leaves the batter lunging,
the knuckleballs dance all over the place.
But then, we lose our focus, maybe,
or the ball just slips in our hand
and we throw a fat one right down the middle
and everything changes just like that.
We know, the second the ball leaves our hand,
it's a bad pitch, but we can't take it back.
We see the batter's eyes grow wide
as his bat comes around in a perfect swing;
we hear the crack of a Louisville Slugger
on stampeding Rawlings horsehide
and all we can do is turn our head,
watch the good innings become as meaningless
as yesterdays flying over the fence.
The only thing we can do is pick up another ball,
throw it up there again, see what happens.

Change

A speaker at a seminar said
that in these uncertain times of Bottom Line
how rare is upward mobility,
you're lucky if you have lateral stability.
A person needs to be prepared to change, he said;
jobs, even careers, at any time,
change houses, change towns,
change states or countries or continents
four or five times or more
during a working lifetime,
you know, like we change underwear,
cars, bars, waistlines, hairlines,
medications, dedications, wars, and whores,
like we change husbands and wives,
even sons and daughters.
My mother told me more than once,
"You'd better change your tune, Mister".

VI

1946

I'd like to believe I was conceived
on a bright July morning,
in the bedroom of a small rented house,
in a little Minnesota town surrounded by cornfields,
a cool breeze billowing the curtains
of an open window,
bringing a meadowlark's song into the room
as my mother and father made newlywed love,
the blankets thrown back on a big twin bed.

My old man, already in his thirties,
was amazed that a woman so pretty
could have chosen him, so footloose back then,
an orphan with no prospects in sight,
when the town was populated with heroes
just returned from the war that he,
due to childhood rheumatic fever, was rejected for.

I'd like to think he went to work that day
with a smile on his face,
while my mother went to cook and waitress
at Grandpa's café in downtown Glencoe,
carrying the seeds of poetry inside the seed that was me,
freshly planted in her womb.

Womb

I cried entering this world,
called by the light,
but grew so accustomed to it
that I now fear the darkness
at the end of life,
though I've heard it said
that darkness calls you with light
to what may be another womb.

Calvary Cemetery, 1962

Adam was in the hole, squaring the corners
while I shoveled dirt away from the grave,
when, of a sudden, old Adam set a senior record
for height and speed as he jumped out of the clay
before a ball of snakes he'd uncovered
could unwind from each other and slither up his leg.
After we both freaked out and caught our breath again,
I went back to cutting grass and trimming around stones.
Adam said he'd finish the hole tomorrow,
hoping the snakes would retreat before the funeral.

After the burial, the grave sealed, sod replaced,
we were able to laugh about it; snakes, man; serpents,
a cluster of raveling reptiles nesting in a Christian cemetery,
and not one of them offering an apple
or the promise of the knowledge of good and evil.
It was probably best Eve had called in sick that day,
given her affinity for sweet-talking serpents,
which many think is what got us into this hole to begin with.

Air Raid Drill

In 1955 we crouched under wooden school desks,
as we prepared for a nuclear attack.
We were told Communists liked to kill Catholics most of all
and had tortures planned for us
worse than the scorching of Lawrence, the stoning of Stephen.
But the real terror occurred when the Monsignor,
the parish dictator, came to drill us on our catechism questions
like "Why did God make you?" or "How do you know God?"
We feared we might be slapped for a wrong answer
as we knelt beside the Monsignor's chair
and we cringed when, after class,
he took Sister Elizabeth into the hallway
and scolded her for our wrong answers.
We heard her whisper, "Yes, Monsignor. No, Monsignor.
I'll do better, Monsignor," probably wishing
she had a desk of her own to crawl under just then,
while Sister Mary Margaret in the classroom next door
drilled the living hell out of her class
like Armageddon was on its way.

As If We Were Not Brothers

May 17.
Today will always be your birthday,
though you'll never be older
than the forty-eight years you were given.
I'm left to wonder if the nineteen years since
would have been enough time for us to seek peace
in the war between us
that began with a goddamn war in Asia
that you were itching to enter,
a war I wanted to flee, but couldn't;
a war, it turned out, that neither of us had to fight,
yet somehow escalated into constant sniping,
senseless battles fought on the home front,
though we managed to maintain a truce of sorts,
a cold war of silence and distance
learned from our father,
as we warily watched each other
across guarded borders we drew in the sand,
both of us too stubborn to wave white flags,
as if we were not brothers.

Today, on the day you'd have been sixty-seven,
I'm left to ponder what peace means
when one side just leaves the battlefield,
killed by time, a common though fickle enemy.
It doesn't mean I won anything, merely having survived.
Maybe we both lost everything.
Though you're gone, I feel like the loser,
no one left to fight but myself,
my own stupid stubbornness, right or wrong,
though right or wrong has no meaning anymore,
except that I've learned there is a way I need to live
and that you never had the time to figure that out,
both of us foolishly obstinate in mutual silence,
as if we were not brothers.

Windstorm

In the eye of the night I lie awake,
half afraid, half in awe of the wind
penetrating every crack in my being.
I think of my brother and his wife
in the next town downwind,
open-eyed and clinging to each other
as the wind that mocks everything
to which we think we're anchored
roars through our lives.
I see them leaning into the gale;
how tightly they must be holding each other,
like roots gripping the soil,
as my brother's cancer blows away his time,
minutes flying off like shingles from a roof;
and I hear the cry in his wife's heart
drowning even the howling outside their walls.
I roll closer to my own wife this night,
circle her in my arms, desperately.

I Bring Three Apples

My brother has the same look in his eyes
as the sick raccoon who has wandered into the yard;
an empty stare, yet somehow focused
on a time and place beyond my seeing.
The raccoon teeters and sways
but does not run at my approach;
its eyes seem to beg me either to help it
or leave it alone in its misery
as it wobbles to the shelter of the woodpile,
the way my brother walks with a cane to his sick bed.
I wonder if it would be more humane to kill the raccoon swiftly,
but instead, I bring three apples and an ear of corn,
lay them within reach of the 'coon's hand-like paws,
though I feel sure I'll find a dead 'coon in the morning.
But at dawn the food is eaten, the raccoon is still breathing,
hunkered into the woodpile like my brother in the bosom of his faith,
where it stays for two days and nights.
On the third morning, the raccoon is gone—
no footprints, no tuft of fur caught on a log,
no trail of blood in the snow to show where it's gone
or who may have carried it away between teeth or talons.
All that remains is the image of those eyes, dark and ringed,
reconciled to the inevitable,
peering at me through a mask of pain and exhaustion.

Preparing for the Dark Season

Yellow aspen leaves fly from their summer homes
like flocks of goldeneyes riding the north wind
as I split and stack red oak logs in perfect rows.
I pull withered brown stalks and vines from frozen garden ground,
rake fallen frost-softened apples from beneath the trees,
seal the house against winter's howl.
I prepare for the dark season
when the earth will take back the green gifts of summer.

My brother prepares for the dark season of sleep
by putting his house on the market,
suddenly too large for a widow to maintain;
he shops with his wife for a smaller place,
easier for her to care for when the time comes.
He totals his insurance benefits and pension funds,
goes over the numbers again and again
to be sure his family will be taken care of when he's gone.
He prepares for his last days
by talking to hospice administrators and funeral directors,
ties up the loose ends of his job
to make the transition easier for his replacement.
He's bought a casket, picked a cemetery plot
where he can sleep well during the dark season.

Tonight, my brother has gathered his loved ones,
tells us he's not afraid, only worried about us left behind.
He tells me he wants a poem at his funeral,
then jokes about whose name he's drawn and who's drawn his
for a Christmas he may not see; but the humor is poignant.
He says the doctors can take care of the pain, he won't suffer;
but there is no doctor for us, for the bittersweet hurt of loving;
and all the firewood in all the forests
won't keep the chill away this winter, this dark season.

My Brother's Eulogy

To help us feel better, I guess,
the priest said
you'd be playing golf,
the game you loved,
on a beautiful course
in heaven.
It's been nineteen years.
Are you any good yet,
get rid of that slice,
putter working?
Are you tired of golf,
rather see your wife
meet your grandchildren?
Eternity goes on forever,
a long time,
even in heaven.

Restoration

My brother's written a poem to remember our father,
a life-time barber, who, when he died,
left behind his old barber chair,
moved with him from shop to shop,
finally coming to rest in the old man's basement,
where he cut the neighbor kids' hair after retiring.
By then, the chair was rusting, its porcelain arms dull,
its leather seat nicked up and cracked like old skin.
The chair swiveled with a groan, the levers squealed,
the foot- and headrests refusing to adjust.

My brother writes a poem with mallets, wrenches, chisels, and files,
sandpaper, grease, and penetrating oil to loosen bound metal;
he writes with new leather, shiny new chrome,
porcelain that gleams like ivory,
levers and gears that turn the chair like a merry-go-round,
raise and lower it like a bumper jack, tilt it like a recliner.
He writes with Dad's old barber tools, found again,
scissors and clippers, metal combs, cleaned up,
that soft brush our dad finished a haircut with,
straight razors and even the old leather strop
our old man slapped to sharpen his razors.

My brother put the chair in the basement of his new house,
and when his brothers come to visit, especially when all together,
we make sure to sit awhile in the restored barber chair,
tell stories about the old man, reminisce, remember him
draping a cloth over our shoulders to keep the hair off of us,
tilting our heads this way, then that, with hands gentle
as only a father's hands could be, shaving the backs of our necks
after the scissors snipped, the clipper hummed in our ears,
dusting us with talcum powder, brushing it off with a soft bristle
    brush,
treating us like his best customers, like we were men who left big tips.
The old man swiveled the 1925 Hanson barber chair under a
    fluorescent light
so we could look in the mirror at a haircut done with love,
seeing him standing behind us like he always did,
still does, though now he's but a memory, a mirage, a poem.

Amputee

Hell, it was only one leg, my father said.
I had two and I can still get around on one
with these crutches and this prosthesis.
It's not the first thing I've ever lost, he said,
thinking back to his parents,
gone before he was five,
his three brothers who all passed away young,
his only daughter, ten days old when she died,
his wife, a couple years ago,
not to mention jobs, time, dignity
lost to the bottle.
What they say about an amputation—
that you can feel a limb after it's removed,
it's true, he said.
This amputated leg still throbs now and then
but no more than the hurts you carry in your heart
when you've lived this long.
The doctors call it phantom pain; it's not.

Disguise

I am a young man
disguised as an old man,
disguised as my father,
my grandfather—
gray beard,
crow's feet,
skin like a coat of old leather.

We're required to wear these old bodies,
these tattered, faded rags,
by cynical gods and goddesses
who've been around too long,
fooling themselves,
coming to us in young peoples' guise—
men as strong as storms,
women pretty as each new dawn,
as if they fear us
for what we tell them of themselves,
their godly egos,
the fading of the rose.

Irregular

Not noticing how the waitresses look at each other,
roll their eyes as I seat myself
on an empty chair at an empty table,
not knowing I've innocently sat
at the "Regular's table" in the local café,
just before the first "Regular"
reaches for his usual chair,
sits down beside me, doesn't say a word,
as if I'm just a misplaced salt shaker,
when the second "Regular" sits down,
then the third, the fourth, the fifth.
They all begin talking at the same time;
no one says a word to me or gives me a glance,
and I finally get the hint, get up, head to the counter,
wondering on which stool I should sit
as I watch as the "Regular's table" fills up,
all but the chair where I sat.
A waitress coyly smiles at me, asks if I'd like coffee,
I say, no thanks, I'd rather have a cup of tea.

Dream Catcher

Three weeks shy of sixty-seven years on earth,
I've just completed my first dream catcher—
a frame of green cottonwood twigs
lashed together with purple thread,
its web woven with the colors of earth and sky.
In its heart a single brown bead is strung,
a wooden spider patiently waiting in her lair
for the web to vibrate with dreams,
sifting them, allowing good dreams to pass through,
trapping, then devouring the malevolent visions
that come to haunt us as we sleep.
I'm three weeks shy of sixty-seven.
May I never cease dreaming.
May my dreams be of the kind the spider lets pass
with a song sung on vibrating strings of light.

Darwin

I tell the old cat,
thin and fragile with age,
sitting on my lap in the sun,
as if he understands English,
that the woman who rescued him,
cleaned him up,
removed the BBs from his hide,
loved him until she died,
is watching us from somewhere,
though I don't know that.
Nobody knows,
though we tell ourselves stories
about a place with golden streets,
a bridge made of a rainbow,
ancestors shining in the night sky,
or that we might come back to live again.
Nobody knows.
What I do know is at this moment
two old guys are sitting together in the sun.

Awakened by a Poem

Before turning on the light
in the stairway
after being awakened by a poem
crying to be written
in the dark of night,
I notice the old gray cat
peering out the window
into darkness
only cats can see through.
He too, must see some kind of poetry
in raindrops
splashing on fallen leaves
which he cannot ignore
any more than I can overlook
what wakes me in the night.

The Jimmy Durante Mantra

I couldn't tell you what I thought about, if anything,
on my morning bike ride up and down the Avon hills,
pedaling in and out of tree-speckled sunshine,
past chirping toads and flashing oriole wings,
a red dragonfly briefly hitching a ride on my bike bag.
All I remember is
Inka dinka do, ka dinka do, ka dinka do
revolving like a rolling wheel in my mind,
a nonsensical mantra, a rhythm for pedaling.
Jimmy Durante is not often thought of as a Zen master,
but, ha cha cha cha cha, why not,
if this mantra propels you over the hills,
unwittingly in search of mystical and mysterious Mrs. Calabash,
whoever and wherever she may be.

Antiques

Scouting for old brass bells
at the antiquery
and finding no collectibles,
I peruse the other customers,
most of whom are antiques themselves
and judging by the cars outside,
worth a lot.

When I look in crystal eyes,
set like stones in wrinkled leather,
I cannot understand
why broken toys and rusty tools
are worth so much
and old people are knickknacks,
not treasured by many.

I look in a foggy, beveled mirror,
see graying hair, crow-foot eyes,
fear a decrease in my own value.

My Buddy's Girlfriend

I once rented a basement house on an old farm
between dead Silver Corners and deader Jakeville
with a couple guys I worked with at the packing plant.
There was a hand pump in the yard for water
and an outhouse out back by the rock pile
where old bottles might be found,
filled with mud and decaying leaves, but unbroken.
What I remember about that basement is this:
I pissed in a fruit jar I kept by the bed,
rather than face that cold outhouse
in the middle of a Minnesota January night.
I put up with the odor until morning,
when I emptied the bottle in a snowbank,
a yellow splotch, like a Charolais bull signing his name.
Suddenly, one morning the outhouse door opened,
you came out cursing the cold,
women can't pee in a jar, you said.
I laughed out loud, wished
you were going back inside to warm up my bed.

Rendezvous at the Apple Dumpling Stand

If we get separated at the State Fair,
if I lose my grip on your hand
amid the crowd of tie-dyed t-shirts,
tattooed bodies and spiky haircuts,
pretty young girls with bare stomachs
and boys wearing baseball caps,
bills facing forward or backward or sideways;
if people wearing saris or burkas
or bib overalls come between us
and we lose each other;
if the sea of shuffling old folks
and mothers and fathers pushing strollers;
if the aroma of deep-fried food,
smoky fireworks or fresh-baked cookies,
the odor of a hundred thousand blossoms
wafting from the horticulture building
or the earthy smells of the animal barns
overwhelms our senses and confounds us;
if the cacophony of conversation,
the pitches of politicians and carny barkers,
the buzz of a hundred thousand people talking at once,
the music of Rasta and polka and old rock 'n roll bands
disorients us,
just go back to the apple dumpling stand,
to the left of the main gate.
I'll be at a picnic table, or maybe you will,
two spoons beside another apple dumpling,
topped with ice cream,
waiting for whichever one of us is not there,
watching, waiting nervously

until one of us comes out of the crowd
and our eyes lock on each other,
our bodies relax again, tension drained.
We'll sit as close to each other as we can
at a sticky picnic table,
jabber about our anxieties, profess our love again
as we dig into an apple dumpling together.

The Company That Misery Loves

Misery shared in raspy harmony,
as we clear our throats,
cough like a Dylan/Dr. John duet,
sung on a scratched record,
played over and over
on a cheap record player with an old needle,
then blow our noses, raw and red,
you in countless Kleenex,
me in a red farmer handkerchief.
We wheeze, sneeze, and sniff like dogs on a hunt,
sinuses so plugged our teeth hurt,
hack up buckets of mucus
from the polluted wells of our lungs.
Our eyes water as we nurse each other
with herbal teas and orange juice,
pills, potions, lotions, and incantations.
Empathetic and sympathetic,
helpless and hopeless,
we're the company that misery loves.

Abiquiu Love Poem

Any day that begins
with horses running across a pasture
to the fence where I stand
with you
is bound to be a good day,
maybe even something more profound
when I see us reflected in their eyes,
proof to me that it's true,
my heart beats,
I breathe,
I am alive here and now,
with you.

Peaches

I pick through April's shrunken woodpile,
throw chips and divots of winter's wood splitting
in the wheelbarrow—box elder chips,
chunks of half-rotted, bone-dry elm,
popple splinters, an odd pine block or two,
all too small or fast-burning
to sate the woodstove's January appetite,
but enough to rekindle a little sunlight,
released in a small fire on a cool morning,
the same way a jar of home-canned peaches releases
the buzz of honeybees on peach blossoms when opened.

I repile oak logs, save them for next winter's cold nights
like jars of sweet peaches, stored on the pantry shelves,
saved for cobbler and pies when the trees are bare.
The thought creeps into my head
that a lot of folks won't see another harvest, another winter.
I hope it's not us, honey; but just in case it is,
let's open a jar of peaches,
savor a hint of summer beside the fire.

Napa Valley Chardonnay

In school
I was taught statistics and facts,
trivia that passes for knowledge;
but I will never know what a dog knows
when it pokes its nose in the snow,
snorting and sniffing, sifting
a story from a scent
in the perfect print of a deer
that was here last night.
Like a pretentious connoisseur,
discerning nostrils flaring
above a cork and glass
of Napa Valley chardonnay,
the dog sniffs as if meditating,
while I just stand there,
head in the air, unaware;
feeling somehow inferior at my inability
to read the tracks of even my own kind,
much less understand the story I inhabit,
the book in which it is written
or the hand that guides the author's pen.

Good-bye, Mojo

Last night we ended your pain,
bid you farewell.
Outside, snow fell in big flakes,
drifting down like fallen leaves.
How you loved the snow;
I picture you covered in new snow,
as if by a quilt,
your nose testing the wind, even in this cold,
then rising, shaking snow from your fur,
your aura released in a sparkling aurora.

This morning I stand alone,
looking out over the tamarack bog
where you liked to run off,
nose to the ground,
when you knew I wasn't looking.
I think of all the times I hollered for you
and you always came back,
so I holler "Mojo, Mojo" as loud as I can,
but the wind takes my words and I swear,
I cry, tears freeze in my beard,
and I feel better and I feel worse
at the same time.

Larry Schug is retired from a life of various kinds of physical labor. He is currently a volunteer writing tutor at the College of St. Benedict and a volunteer naturalist at St. John's University Outdoor University. He lives with his wife, a dog, and two cats near a large tamarack bog in St. Wendel Township, Minnesota. Larry is the author of seven books of poems–*Scales Out of Balance* (1990), *Caution: Thin Ice* (1993), *The Turning of Wheels* (2001), *Arrogant Bones* (2008), *Nails* (2011), and *At Gloaming* (2014) all published by North Star Press of St. Cloud, Minnesota, and a chapbook, *Obsessed with Mud*, published by Poetry Harbor, Duluth, Minnesota. *Caution: Thin Ice* was a 1993 Minnesota Book Award finalist and *Arrogant Bones* was a 2008 Midwest Book Award finalist. Larry has won three Central Minnesota Arts Board grants and was awarded a 2008 McKnight Fellowship for Writers.

CPSIA information can be obtained
at www.ICGtesting.com
Printed in the USA
LVOW12s1325060317
526275LV00004B/5/P